For Dee,

Wishing you many smiles
& happy thoughts!

Love,
Michael

To all the furry felines out there who are up to no good

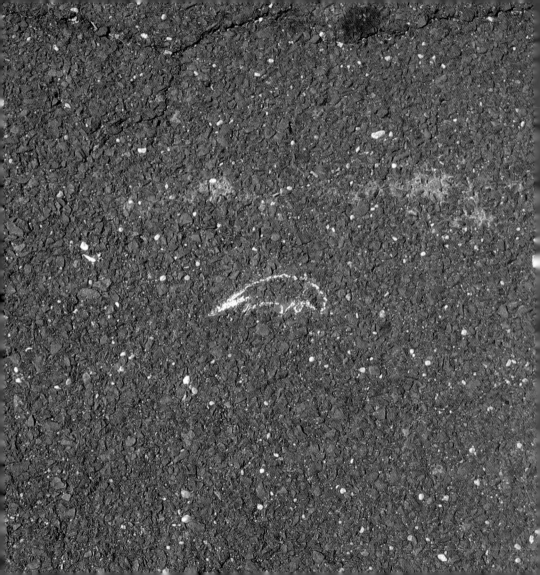

FELINE FELONS

Caught in the Act

Debbie Keller
Designed by Diane Hobbing

Ariel Books
**Andrews McMeel
Publishing**
Kansas City

Photos courtesy of Marjorie Hoffmann, Tracee Williams, Jean Knecht, Sandy and Doug Brubaker, Charlie Groff, the Strickler Family (Scott, Michelle, Greg, and Bryan), Bob Egan, PictureQuest, Stockbyte, Photodisc, and Photos.com.

06 07 08 09 10 TWP 10 9 8 7 6 5 4 3 2 1

ISBN-13: 978-0-7407-5726-6
ISBN-10: 0-7407-5726-1

Library of Congress Control Number: 2005933903

www.andrewsmcmeel.com

FELINE FELONS

Copyright Infringement

Fashion police arrested Tina G. after illegally reproducing designer hand-bags and selling them as Kitty Koats on the Internet.

Suspect was cited for napping in the public way. The suspect, a card-carrying member of the American Feline Liberties Union, is suing the city for discrimination of narcoleptics.

Obstruction of Sidewalk

DEN

Case No _____

Time of Collectio ____

Mittens F. was caught red-handed holding her victim by its tail. Mittens claimed she was only borrow-ing the victim to show her owner in return for a good chin tickle.

Attempted Kidnapping

AIN OF CUSTODY

From _____

Date _____

By _____
Time _____

By _____
Time _____

By _____
Time _____

Lily T. was arrested for offering the dog shiatsu massages for an entire year if he promised not to tell it was she who knocked off the parakeet.

Bribery of a Witness

Illegal Gambling

"I give you four-to-one odds I beat this rap. Double your bet and I'll toss in a Fluffy Muffy's Black Leather Studded Collar His and Her Gift Set."

A nanny cam caught Tabby W. in the act of helping himself to leftover tuna casserole while his owners were at work.

Burglary

Suspect was cited after spending three days on a fourth-story window ledge unnerving passersby below.

Loitering

EVIDENCE INVENTORY RECORD

NAME OF CLIENT
BFI Investigator:
OBTAINED FROM:
BFI Investigator:
PROPERTY STORED

DESCRIPTION OF PR

Paw prints
identified
Virgil K. as
the lap cat
who stole
women's hearts
and men's
wallets.

Pickpocketing

CHAIN OF CUSTODY:

DATE OBTAINED	RECEIVED BY (SIGNATURE/PRINT)	ITEMS RECEIVED	REASON FOR CHANG OF CUSTODY

Suspect was charged with the illegal disposal of animal remains after stuffing the carcasses of unlucky mice between logs in the woodpile.

Illegal Dumping

Attempted Murder in the First Degree

Muffy E. was charged with attempted murder when all three potential victims identified her as the cat who flipped the switch. Muffy was unaware that blenders need a power supply to operate, thus her murder plans were foiled.

Parole Violation

POLICE REPORT

Parole Violation

Pattycakes R. was arrested for violating the terms of her parole. Originally convicted of cruelty to children and breaking and entering a vending machine, Pattycakes now faces banishment from the house and thirty days without a saucer of cream.

Trespassing

Boo-Boo D. was cited for tres-passing after a stranger came home to find him doing yoga in her favorite chair.

Suspect was arrested for insider trading after auctioning off a chinchilla's coat two days before she was to be given away.

Insider Trading

Purse Snatching

EVIDENCE

Agency

OUS SIGNS

Case No

Time of Collection

Suspect was caught on
video camera sweetly
nuzzling Grandma's legs
while the old lady
extracted cash from an
ATM. After her trans-
action, Grandma bent
down to pet the kitty,
and the suspect stole
her purse.

AIN OF CUSTODY

By

Time

By

Time

By

Time

From

Date

Neville K. was apprehended for stalking and terrorizing a pet gerbil. Now on permanent lockout, Neville continues to display stalking behavior in the presence of leaves, twigs, and dandelions. Psychiatric evaluation has been ordered.

Stalking

Malicious Disfigurement

"If you ask me, I did that lizard a favor.
She looks much better without her tail.
And think of how much weight she lost
thanks to me!"

". . . and bring
a salmon fillet
to the dock at
midnight or
you'll never see
your canary
again."

Kidnapping

Duke L. was sentenced to house arrest after attacking a police officer and running off with his toupee. "I thought it was a squirrel," claimed Duke.

Assault on an Officer

EVIDENCE INVENTORY RECORD

NAME OF CLIENT
BFI Investigator:
OBTAINED FROM:
BFI Investigator:
PROPERTY STORED

DESCRIPTION OF PR

"All I did was
take one little
schlip. I mean
sip."

Drunk and Disorderly

CHAIN OF CUSTODY:

DATE OBTAINED	RECEIVED BY (SIGNATURE/PRINT)	ITEMS RECEIVED	REASON FOR CHANG OF CUSTODY

Deadbeat Dad

Shiloh S. was cited for failure to pay child support after it was discovered he used the funds to support his habit of compulsive hoarding.

Identity Theft

Suspect was apprehended while trying to purchase $2,500 worth of cat food with a credit card and identification issued to one Fido.

Possession of Stolen Goods

POLICE REPORT

Possession of Stolen Goods

Authorities were called after Chuck W.'s owners discovered their centerpiece missing from their annual holiday party. Both Chuck and the mini tree were found later that day in the crawl space under the house. Also found was a doll's sock with the letter C on it, a saucer of milk, and a cookie.

Impersonating an Officer

Seamus T. was charged when he was found sitting in the front seat of Sergeant O'Doole's patrol vehicle. "I thought it was O'Doole until I saw those pointy ears," said O'Doole's partner.

Contempt of Court

"I didn't mean
to claw my way
up the judge's
leg. It was just a
Pavlovian response.
From where I was
sitting his robes
looked like
curtains and
I just reacted."

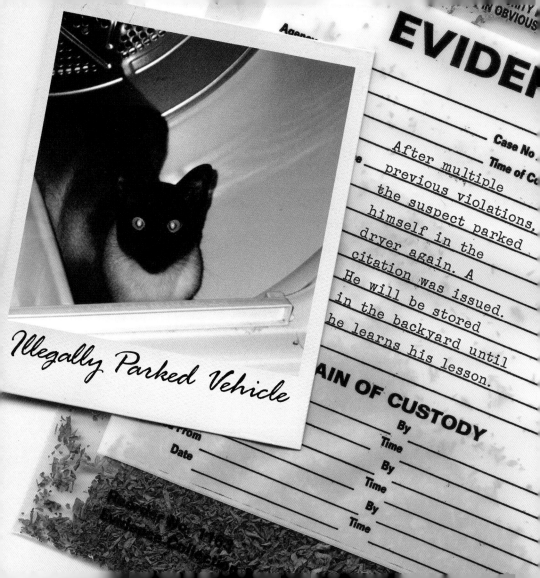

Illegally Parked Vehicle

EVIDEN

Case No.

Time of Co

After multiple previous violations, the suspect parked himself in the dryer again. A citation was issued. He will be stored in the backyard until he learns his lesson.

AIN OF CUSTODY

By
Time
By
Time
By
Time
By
Time

From
Date

Suspect was apprehended for solicitation of heavy petting from an undercover officer.

Lewd Solicitation

Fraud

Suspect was charged with fraud after posing as a pet psychic and bilking dozens of neighborhood cats out of kitty treats and milk money.

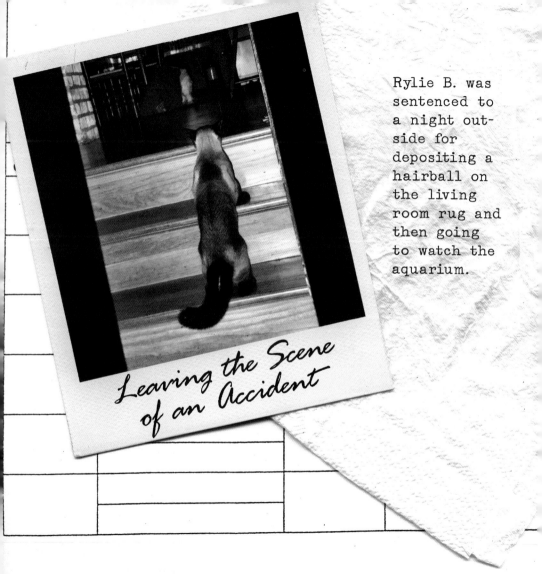

Rylie B. was sentenced to a night outside for depositing a hairball on the living room rug and then going to watch the aquarium.

Leaving the Scene of an Accident

Suspect cited for verbally assaulting owner. Apparently suspect was angry that dinner was not served on time.

Verbal Assault

EVIDENCE INVENTORY RECORD

NAME OF CLIENT
BFI Investigator:
OBTAINED FROM:
BFI Investigator:
PROPERTY STORED

DESCRIPTION OF PR

Stumpy P. was
arrested for
attempting to
steal a sausage
off his owner's
plate while said
owner was get-
ting a beer.

Attempted Robbery

CHAIN OF CUSTODY:

DATE OBTAINED	RECEIVED BY (SIGNATURE/PRINT)	ITEMS RECEIVED	REASON FOR CHANGE OF CUSTODY

Two pet rats identified suspect as the cat who eavesdropped on their escape plans. Apparently she wanted to intercept and eat them.

Illegal Wiretapping

Adultery

Sparky R. was charged with adultery when his mate walked in on him spooning with her sister.

SIGNATURE OF PERSON F.

RESIDENCE OF PERSON FING

DATE   SIGNATURE OF O

EMPLOYER AND ADDRESS

REASON FINGERPRINTED

LEAVE

NFO
ST M

R

Destruction of Public Property

1. R. THUMB

2. R. IND

3. R. MIDDLE

4. R. RING

6. L. THUMB

7. L. INDEX

POLICE REPORT

Destruction of Public Property

Suspect was cited for excessively clawing a fence in the city park. Under interrogation the suspect broke down and confessed to other municipal crimes, including using the playground as a litter box and eating the golf course when her bulimia got out of control.

Trafficking in Stolen Property

Suspect was apprehended for stealing light-bulbs from a local hardware store and selling them as memory enhancers to dim-witted canines.

Suspect was caught stealing yarn from a crafts store. The suspect claimed she was hired to crochet an afghan for the store's display, but officers knew without an opposable thumb, she couldn't crochet. Or knit.

Shoplifting

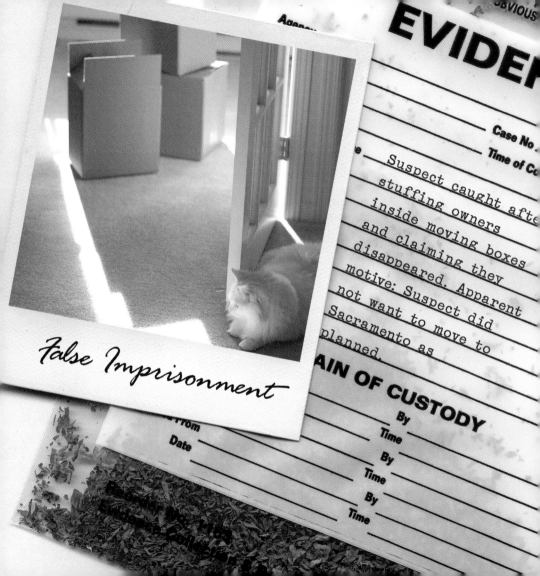

False Imprisonment

EVIDEN

OBVIOUS

Agenc

Case No.

Time of Co

e

Suspect caught afte

stuffing owners

inside moving boxes

and claiming they

disappeared. Apparent

motive: Suspect did

not want to move to

Sacramento as

planned.

AIN OF CUSTODY

By

From

Time

Date

By

Time

By

Time

By

Time

Hercules D., catnip leaves clinging to his tail, was cited after he was found hunting, feeding, and trying to mate with a pair of socks.

Under the Influence of a Controlled Substance

Cruelty to Animals

Peaches P. videotaped herself eating a daddy longlegs spider as an audition piece for the hit TV show *Phobia Factor*, but the tape ended up in the hands of the wrong authorities.

Rusty W. was apprehended when his girlfriend identified his pheromones as those of the cat who'd been marking the neighborhood.

Tagging

Suspect was caught peering into the children's room while their gecko was shedding her skin.

Peeping Tom

EVIDENCE INVENTORY RECORD

NAME OF CLIENT	
BFI Investigator:	
OBTAINED FROM:	
BFI Investigator:	
PROPERTY STORED	

DESCRIPTION OF PR

"This is what Bob's in the slammer for? This is a salt and battery, not assault and battery! He was framed! It was that jealous hamster who set him up! Well, maybe she'll just have a little accident with the dog tonight."

Assault and Battery

CHAIN OF CUSTODY:

DATE OBTAINED	RECEIVED BY (SIGNATURE/PRINT)	ITEMS RECEIVED	REASON FOR CHANGE OF CUSTODY

Angry neighbors called police at 4 A.M. to complain about loud cat wails coming from a nearby alley. Suspect was found dancing the rumba.

Disturbing the Peace

Breaking and Entering

Stormy B. was found in the living room after having been locked outside. "I was doing chin-ups on the window screen when it popped right off," said Stormy. "I thought I'd been invited in."

Tampering with Evidence

POLICE REPORT

Tampering with Evidence

Suspect was apprehended with feathers poking out of her mouth after authorities discovered Exhibit A missing from her own funeral.

(Exhibit A is a small finch whose lifeless body was found on the mat by the kitchen door. Her demise is still under investigation.)

Assault with Intent to Commit Mayhem

"I'm innocent, I tell you. Innocent! It's not my fault I pierced that lady's ears when I fell from the tree. Hasn't anyone heard of the righting reflex? I can't help but land feet first!"

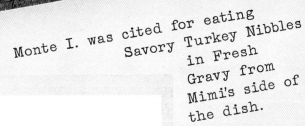
Monte I. was cited for eating Savory Turkey Nibbles in Fresh Gravy from Mimi's side of the dish.

Taking Property without Right

Intimidating a Witness

EVIDEN

Case No

Time of Co

Cleo P. was arreste
for threatening to
pan-fry Flicker
should Flicker feel
compelled to tell
authorities about
Cleo's midnight fish-
ing habit and the
disappearance of her
roommates.

AIN OF CUSTODY

By

Time

By

Time

By

Time

"I'm asking you, is this the face of a cat who would intentionally toss a sweet, innocent little guinea pig from a three-story building? I swear to you, she just fell."

Murder in the First Degree

Aiding and Abetting a Criminal

Zinc N. turned in his partner when he discovered the cat had eaten both mourning doves nesting in the backyard. "One was supposed to be mine," said Zinc, thus incriminating himself.

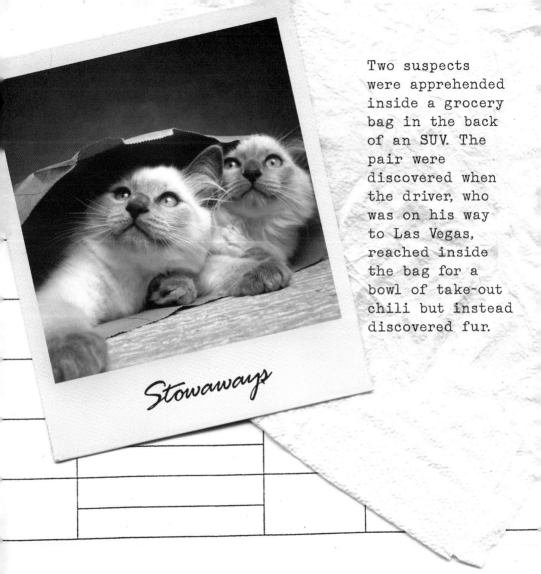

Stowaways

Two suspects were apprehended inside a grocery bag in the back of an SUV. The pair were discovered when the driver, who was on his way to Las Vegas, reached inside the bag for a bowl of take-out chili but instead discovered fur.

"All I did was ask for seven cans of tuna to stop spraying the bathroom rug. Since when is having a big appetite a crime?"

Extortion

NAME OF CLIENT
BFI Investigator:
OBTAINED FROM:
BFI Investigator:
PROPERTY STORED

DESCRIPTION OF PR

Suspect escaped after being charged with stealing three Kumonryu koi from a backyard pond. It's believed he's headed to Japan on a yacht purchased with proceeds from the stolen goods.

Escape from Custody

CHAIN OF CUSTODY:

DATE OBTAINED	RECEIVED BY (SIGNATURE/PRINT)	ITEMS RECEIVED	REASON FOR CHANG OF CUSTODY

"Hey, it's not my fault I'm a stud muffin. So I forgot to mention I was married once, or several times. It's not like I can fit a gold band on my claw or anything."

Bigamy

Terrorism

Suspect charged with intention-ally sleeping on the dog's bed for the sole purpose of depositing fleas.

Slander

"Pssst. See the person holding this book? They were at the SPCA last week trying to get a peek at some tail. What a Peeping Tom. Their picture should be in here."

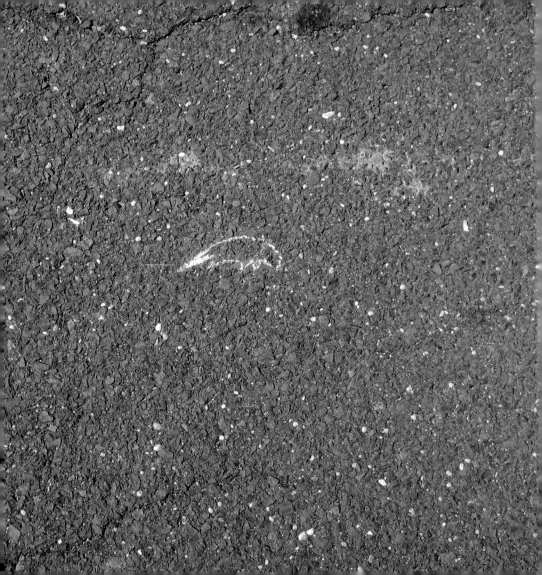